Lofts

Lofts

ROCKPORT

PUBLISHERS

Editor: Aurora Cuito

Texts: Ana Cristina G. Cañizares

Graphic Design: Emma Termes Parera

Layout: Gisela Legares Gili

Copyright for the international edition:

© H Kliczkowski-Onlybook, S.L.

La Fundición, 15. Polígono Industrial Santa Ana

28529 Rivas-Vaciamadrid. Madrid

Ph.: +34 91 666 50 01

Fax: +34 91 301 26 83

onlybook@onlybook.com

www.onlybook.com

Copyright for the US edition:

© 2004 by Rockport Publishers, Inc.

Published in the United States of America by

Rockport Publishers, Inc.

33 Commercial Street

Gloucester, Massachusetts 01930-5089

Tel.: (978) 282-9590

Fax: (978) 283-2742

www.rockpub.com

Library of Congress Cataloging-in-Publication Data available

ISBN: 1-59253-057-5

10 9 8 7 6 5 4 3 2

Printed in Singapore

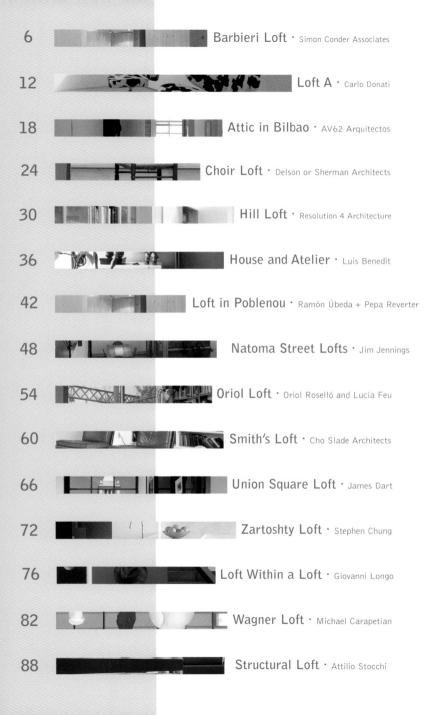

BARBIERI LOFT

Architect: Simon Conder Associates
Location: London, United Kingdom
Photography: Peter Warren

The clients, a journalist and a photographer, acquired this loft on the second floor of a nineteenth-century industrial building. The objective was to create spacious and bright areas that communicated well with each other. This was especially important between the kitchen and the living room so conversation could be facilitated between those cooking and the guests.

Ample storage space was also required, and the studio had to be separated from the living quarters. Given the limited surface area, the key decision was made not to subdivide the space but rather, to have a unified atmosphere.

The bathroom is made of wood except for the sides of the shower, which are made of panes of translucent glass.

Architect: Carlo Donati
Location: Milan, Italy
Photography: Mateo Piazza

Originally, this space was divided up into two small apartments, one on the top floor and the other on the bottom floor. The one on the bottom floor was connected, by means of a corridor, to a spacious area which served as an art gallery. Now, a spiral staircase emerges from the first floor and leads to the bedrooms on the second floor.

The second staircase leads to the master suite which is complete with a bathroom, wardrobe, and direct access to the interior of the garden. The rooms on the first floor have interior and exterior spaces and receive direct natural light.

14

Samarcanda stone is used in the design of the bathroom. It is part of the relaxation area and was designed to be integrated into the living room area.

Architect: AV62 Arquitectos
Location: Bilbao, Spain
Photography: Susana Arechaga and Luis Ambrós

This loft is situated inside an eighteenth-century building in the old section of Bilbao, Spain, and exhibits the scars of many renovations and years of weathering.

The existing framework of wood beams and structural columns were maintained, eliminating unnecessary divisions, to facilitate the entry of light and the distribution of space.

The bathroom is easily accessed from the bedroom or the living room, as is the storage space located on the other side of the partition.

Architect: Delson or Sherman Architects
Location: Brooklyn, NY, United States
Photography: Catherine Tighe

This warehouse was converted into a church in the 1930s. Architects bought the neglected property and transformed it into a home for a family of four. The space was gutted out, although even the shell was in need of repair. Major structural work included rebuilding an exterior wall and bolstering existing trusses with new heavy-timber struts and steel plates.

In order to emphasize the vastness of the two-story volume, a series of deep skylights that spill light into the space were installed into the ceiling. The room was furnished with a giant 20-foot table and long bookcases.

The mezzanine, which was previously the church's choir loft, is an intimate living area and shelters another sitting area underneath, offering cozy alternatives to the big room.

HILL LOFT

Architect: Resolution 4 Architecture
Location: New York, NY, United States
Photography: Eduard Hueber

This loft is situated in a building with an industrial past in the emerging New York TriBeCa neighborhood. It is an example of a proficient response to the requirements of space.

One of the walls that runs the length of the apartment was completely outfitted with built-in closets and shelves. The design reflects the three different living areas. The shelves for the television, books and decorative elements, and the kitchen cabinets, afford ample space for storing and keeping objects. Different steel columns are inserted into the wall of built-ins which visually separate the three areas: bedroom, kitchen-dining room, and living room.

Architect: Luis Benedit
Location: Buenos Aires, Argentina
Photography: Jordi Miralles

This loft was previously a bakery that was part of an old market. It belongs to Luis Benedit, a well-known artist and architect who has exhibited his work in the New York Museum of Modern Art and the Contemporary Art Museum in Sydney, Australia. He decided to buy the 1,830 square-foot space and transform it into his own living and working space.

To create a more homey atmosphere, the owner coated the walls with panels of Guatambú wood. He also introduced a quartz lighting system along the industrial ceiling grill.

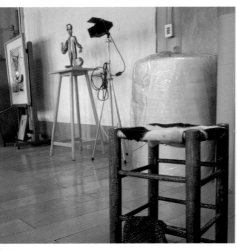

The kitchen can be seen through a dilapidated wall on the far end, which was left intact, and the countertop was made from tiles that were found at a demolition site.

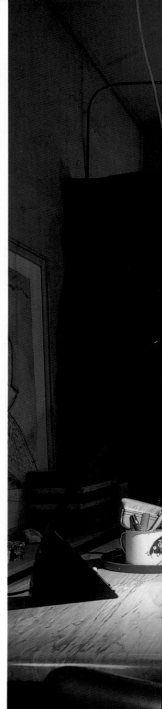

Architects: Ramón Úbeda and Pepa Reverter
Location: Barcelona, Spain
Photography: Pere Planells

According to the architects, this space allowed for an easy renovation. Their aim in every residential project is to achieve spaciousness and light. The finished loft offered more than 3,000 square feet of clear and open space that most conventional homeowners do not enjoy.

Massive windows occupy the perimeter of the loft, flooding the interior with natural light. A continuous resin pavement covers the floors, bouncing the light up into every corner.

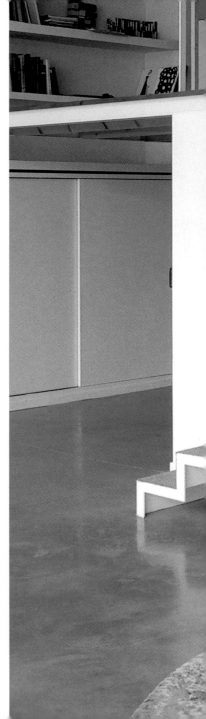

The mixture of styles can be seen in the bathrooms in which one is more minimalist, using wood and translucent glass, and the other is more personalized, with an amusing tile pattern imitated by the piles of books on the floor.

Architect: Jim Jennings
Location: San Francisco, CA, United States
Photography: Roger Casas

The renovation of this rectangular two-story space led to the creation of a mezzanine level on which the bedroom is situated. A translucent glass balcony looks from the bedroom onto the living area underneath.

Steel is one of the primary resources used in this project to accomplish a modern yet raw effect throughout the loft.

The dining area faces the kitchen and is separated by an island. The concrete floors and radiant heat provide an efficient means of living comfortably within this space.

ORIOL LOFT

Architects: Oriol Roselló and Lucía Feu
Location: Barcelona, Spain
Photography: Jordi Miralles

An old textile factory situated in the Barcelona Eixample district was converted into a block of flats a few years ago. The architect Oriol Roselló kept the ground floor of the building, the only part which preserved the original industrial past of the building such as the forged, trellis-iron beams.

The rooms of the dwelling open out to two patios, the larger becomes an improvised living room and dining room when the nice weather arrives. It opens off of the great living room-library. The other one which is much smaller comes off the kitchen, studio, and the bedroom.

The dressing room consists of two pieces of furniture between the living room and the bedroom. Leaning against one of the pieces of furniture is a mat that serves as an improvised guest bed.

Architect: Cho Slade Architects
Location: New York, NY, United States
Photography: Jordi Miralles

The clients of this project, a father and his two children, commissioned Cho Slade studio to re-model their Manhattan apartment. One of the main requirements was that the plan be open. In spite of such a flexible request, the two existing rooms in the center of the loft were to be left intact for the children.

The rectangular floor plan of the loft is divided into three parts: the central part is used for dining; the southern part is occupied by a large play area and an alcove for the father; and the northern part houses a diaphanous living room.

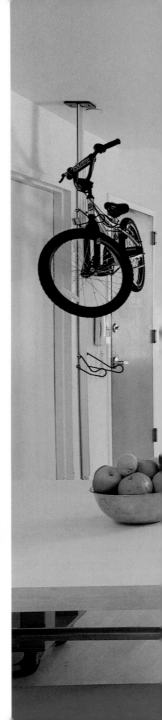

The electrical wires were installed in the false ceiling over the central part of the loft, which reduces the usable height of the dwelling by a few centimeters.

Architect: James Dart
Location: New York City, NY, United States
Photography: Catherine Tighe

Occupying the oblique corner of 4th Avenue and 12th Street, this loft's irregular geometry inspired the architects to create a series of framed views of the city.

The decoration is restrained, though not minimalist, and favors the use of symmetry and neutral colors.

A small reading area behind the living room can be transformed into a guest bedroom by pulling out the floor-to-ceiling sliding panels and convertible bed hidden inside the wall.

The new design incorporates a central core composed of the kitchen and bathroom. This provides uninterrupted views of the exterior through the perimeter windows. The stairs along the side lead to the mezzanine level, which houses a small library and the master bedroom beyond.

ZARTOSHTY LOFT

Architect: Stephen Chung
Location: Boston, MA, United States
Photography: Eric Roth

Located on the top floor of a new artist loft building in downtown Boston, this project involved the conversion of a 2,400-square-foot raw shell into a primary residence.

At the owner's request, the architect designed a two-story living/dining area, an open kitchen, a wet bar, and a media room. A staircase, partly concealed behind a tall cupboard unit, leads to the upper mezzanine, which is designated to be the master bedroom, bathroom, and study.

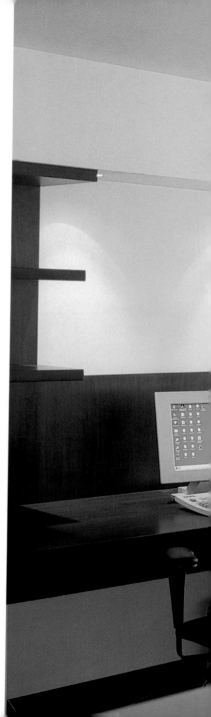

Architect: Giovanni Longo
Location: Milan, Italy
Photography: Andrea Martiradonna

In what was once the site of the Schlumberger factory, this attic space was rehabilitated into a living space for a young professional. The rectangular space has a 23-foot-high ceiling. The entrance is located at one extreme, and though there is only one facade, the loft receives abundant light from a pitched glass ceiling.

The living room occupies the central area. A chimney that pierces the ceiling delineates the kitchen and dining areas, which rest underneath a lowered ceiling that stops short of either side in order to let light from the glass ceiling pass through.

A steel staircase, lightweight in comparison to the chimney, leads to the bedroom, which is sheltered inside an independent structure for ultimate privacy and an escape from daily routine. As if it were a house inside a house, as the architects refer to it, the glass catwalk that leads to the bedroom isolates it further from the surrounding area.

Architect: Michael Carapetian
Location: Venice, Italy
Photography: Andrea Martiradonna

This residence was inserted into an industrial shell constructed in 1910 and known as the Dreher Brewery. The aim of the architect was to keep the structure intact by introducing new surfaces to sustain the rooms without removing any of the existing brick walls and wood trusses.

The terraces and the lowest level of the loft are raised by a suspended steel floor and a suspended steel-frame wall that divides the space from the rest of the enveloping structure. An ellipse-shaped wood platform is cantilevered from two wood structural plates, taking up one-third of the space. This ellipse is composed of prefabricated plywood box-beams.

The outdoor area consists of wooden decks, paths, and small ponds of water; an ideal place to relax and enjoy the views of distant Venice.

STRUCTURAL LOFT

Architect: Attilio Stocchi
Location: Bergamo, Italy
Photography: Andrea Martiradonna

Given the extraordinary height of the ceilings in this loft, the architect decided to take advantage of the extra space and incorporate an additional level.

The loft is broken up by thirteen steel posts distributed in asymmetrical clusters around the space. These posts support the horizontal plane system to create the sensation of instability. They pierce through whatever comes in their way in an arbitrary manner.

The upper level consists of walkways flanked in glass that lead to the bathroom and bedroom. The use of glass to protect the catwalk ensures transparency and the flow of light throughout both levels of the loft. This passage not only links areas but also serves to close in the living area just underneath, acting as a lowered ceiling to provide a more intimate atmosphere.